NORTHERN SPY

NORTHERN SPY

Poems by Chase Twichell

University of Pittsburgh Press

Published by the University of Pittsburgh Press, Pittsburgh, Pa. 15260
Copyright © 1981, P. Chase Twichell
All rights reserved
Feffer and Simons, Inc., London
Manufactured in the United States of America

Library of Congress Cataloging in Publication Data

Twichell, Chase
  Northern spy.

  (Pitt poetry series)
  I. Title.
PS3570.W47N6   811'.54   80-54061
ISBN 0-8229-3437-X   AACR2
ISBN 0-8229-5328-5 (pbk.)

Acknowledgment is made to the following publications, which first published some of the poems in this book: *Crazy Horse, Field, Ploughshares, Poetry Now, Quarry West, raccoon,* and *A Review.*

"Watercress and Ice" first appeared in the June 1978 issue of *Antaeus* and is reprinted with permission. "Geode," "Holy Night," and "When the Rapture Comes, I Will Depart Earth" were originally published in *The Chariton Review.* "The Dark Hinges" originally appeared in *The Georgia Review.* "The Iris, That Sexual Flower" was first published in *The Ohio Review.* "The North" first appeared in *Portland Review.* "A Stone from the Bottom," "Sisters," "This Was a Farm," "Three Dreams of Disaster," and "Your Eightieth" were originally published in *Prairie Schooner.*

*The publication of this book is supported by grants
from the National Endowment for the Arts
in Washington, D.C., a Federal agency,
and the Pennsylvania Council on the Arts.*

To my kindred spirit, the photographer.

Sprouts from the original tree were taken up and planted by Roswell Humphrey and by him the first fruit of the Northern Spy was raised as the original tree died before bearing.

—from *The Apples of New York,*
Report of the New York Agricultural
Experiment Station, 1903

It is an extreme evil to depart from the company of the living before you die.

—Seneca

CONTENTS

CONTENTS

NORTHERN
SPY

INLAND

Above the blond prairies,
the sky is all color and water.
The future moves
from one part to another.

This is a note
in a tender sequence
that I call love,
trying to include you,
but it is not love.
It is music, or time.

To explain the pleasure I take
in loneliness, I speak of privacy,
but privacy is the house around it.
You could look inside,
as through a neighbor's window
at night, not as a spy
but curious and friendly.
You might think
it was a still life you saw.

Somewhere, the ocean
crashes back and forth
like so much broken glass,
but nothing breaks.
Against itself,
it is quite powerless.

Irises have rooted
all along the fence,
and the barbed berry-vines
gone haywire.

Unpruned and broken,
the abandoned orchard
reverts to the smaller,
harder fruits, wormy and tart.
In the stippled shade,
the fallen pears move
with the soft bodies of wasps,
and cows breathe in
the licorice silage.

It is silent
where the future is.
No longer needed there,
love is folded away in a drawer
like something newly washed.
In the window,
the color of the pears intensifies,
and the fern's sporadic dust
darkens the keys of the piano.

Clouds containing light
spill out my sadness.
They have no sadness of their own.

The timeless trash of the sea
means nothing to me —
its roaring descant,
its multiple concussions.
I love painting more than poetry.

19 LAKE STREET

At last the maples
throw off their soft red buds,
and the neighbors emerge
to scrape the lawns.
New mothers wheel their offspring
up and down over the curbs,
absorbed by the awkwardness.
And which of all the elements
is the strangest?
The little spirits struggling
in their yellow blankets,
the huge trees falling to pieces?
The dismantled, oily parts
of a machine laid out on rags
like a metal picnic?
A curtain shivers. Someone is watching
the tulips enlarge in the gardens.
They force their closed,
still colorless flowers
up out of the bare dirt.

A STONE FROM THE BOTTOM

There is no vocabulary
for the dream,
the baby in a rage.

A man leaves cursive
rib marks on my skin;
love, that printing press,

closes down for sleep.
At first I'm on the doctor's table
mouthing off, making noise.

I can locate no wounds
though I break with blood.
It's twins, a tiny man

with no head,
a boy with a slingshot
killing squirrels.

Cold water slicks my hair back.
Sidestroke, I make
for the boats that

knock each other in the arms
of the storm, lashed tight
with tarpaulins.

In sleep this man mimics
the language of the dream,
thirsty and turning,

calling for home, the bath,
the weightless time.
I dive through a green zone.

Clean water eases me
awake; the sidelong fish
in their deep houses

fin into nothing.
A stone from the bottom
proves I remember him.

Come up for the air of his kiss
and the cold depth
of my dream wavers.

But outside, in the courtyard
under the ghostly laundry:
a baby carriage with a noise inside.

SISTERS

In Mother's pearls and nightgown
you'd trail the slippery cloth along the floor,
talking to yourself. In all your wild wishes
the yards of silk would slide and unwind,
and the crown send out its white light.
Five years old, shadow, overlap,
you'd rock in your bed on hands and knees,
ramming the pillow, fraying the hair
on your forehead. You'd beat out a song,
rocking to sleep.

Snow sifts down
through our childhood, pale screen.
Behind it, a dog at the door, scratching;
you in my outgrown clothes,
flat-chested and graceful;
thunderstorms in the old house,
a black flood of sky;
random sparks, the static crackle,
brushing our hair out in the dark.

You move into a house I've never seen,
with a wind chime in the kitchen
and a screen door that sticks.
You live among easels, dented tubes,
a skylight, the smell of clay,
no longer the child inheriting headaches
or waiting till Christmas for the harp:
pink rubber strings and a toy sound.

And this man, at home in your studio,
acts like a husband
with his rolled-up sleeves,
moving your worktable,
resting his hand on your back.
He was our father in the dream
before you knew him.
He will be your sons.

Snow falls between us,
room of white laundry,
hushing the voices: familiar, lost.
Cedar and mothballs, the attic with its
passages, raw boards full of nail punctures:
closed off. Boxes marked *Liza's baby clothes,*
that handwriting: given away.
Even the dog that snapped
and pulled back its black lips
to protect you, almost forgotten:
jingle of licences, chains on the road.

In this blank night,
you are going home,
driving through the slow, total avalanche
that turns you back into the spiral,
fleece-thick, white as milk.
It will sing you its
own last wish for itself,
the windshield wipers rubbing
their arcs against the glass,
signaling their goodbye.

You soak your brushes
in the last of the turpentine,
and linger by the window
in a T-shirt and shorts.
You rock a little, eyes closed,
and the small shadows of your face
suggest the child bones, almost.

Planes of light fall down around you.
In the shuttered house, on the stairs:
remember? The heavy banister,
the slippery sound of costumes,
rain blowing the curtain back.

A MYSTERIOUS HEART

I don't like what the world has become.
At night, the sprinklers sound like rain
but I am neither fooled nor consoled.

Real rain no longer exists,
and the fish in the rivers
flash with phosphorus.

In secret I compile the history
of the world before the tragedy,
a lonely occupation. As a foreigner,

I write in a language of immunity,
make notes of things, deciphering,
invisible as a tourist.

Inside the nebulous skies,
millions of tiny planes
disperse their seed,

and the radio calls it weather.
There was weather in my childhood
on the other planet,

not that it was lovely. It was cold.
It was lovely, but cold.
When, in my investigations,

I search through the scrapbooks
for proof of this,
I discover the pictures, six to a page,

entangled in a white trellis,
the space around them.
This is the way I remember

Father's house, a square of darkness
crisscrossed by the moon,
a latticework the ivy climbed.

That's me in the window,
wondering about love.
I had a mysterious heart.

Perhaps my present disorientation
began on such a night.
In the many layers of the sky,

the stars appeared to swim
and multiply, like snow, or sperm,
or the white cells of death

on the laboratory slide.
Or maybe it was Christmas,
and other people had the Spirit,

but I never had it, as far as I know.
But all childhoods are hazardous,
and their cruelties ordinary.

I love the snowfall,
the blossoms of silence
that gather around us.

Then this planet is cast as the other,
and my life as another's.
The planes dive toward terra firma

with ice on their wings, which is justice,
their cockpits full of moonlight.
So whether the water spills

through the pipes and spigots
or freezes in the heavens,
it makes no difference.

I come from the snowbound planet,
so far away it seems a spark,
a chip of ice. The truth is,

I did not consent to exile here.
So the mind goes into the past,
or up into a clean, new galaxy.

THE WATER CARRIER

He knelt, and dipped his twin buckets.
The river, thickened with dust,
lagged at its banks,

and the papery rushes turned green.
The yoke and his shoulder were one bone.
Barefoot, he carried water past houses

where the tile was too beautiful a blue,
and women stirred in airy gauze.
Oxen cut their hoof marks on the road.

He watched the horses, groomed and rippling,
pass through the heat.
He kept his thin frame forever.

Dust in its lethargy rose and fell
and rose between heaven and earth,
where he was alone.

NITROUS OXIDE

If the dentist speaks to you,
he knows you will not answer.
He is drilling on the far side
of the brain, in another room.

You suck in each dessicating breath
through a mask of black rubber,
the striated blinds
slicing the window light

like the fronds of a tree in paradise,
that expensive hotel.
Down the hall a man yells
with rage, drink, or illness.

Or he is one side
of your parents' lifelong argument,
with sex in the grand old style,
fervent as worship seems

in a foreign language,
laden with postures and specified acts.
God knows there is no going back
on a heart locked

into that fatal prayer.
A green car slides forward,
showered with jewels from the car wash.
It will drive you to your wedding

and home again. So, you have fainted.
The grass is spiked with dew,
and a tiny fountain bursts
into a glass of water, which you drink.

The nurses are the crowd
that caught you when you fell.
Their voices come and go,
as if between stations.

A bottle leaks into the black hose
into your lungs. The vapor contains
a parade of little parents, bearing
the traits for intelligence and sadness

like so many colorless flags.
But they have always been there.
As you have been here,
drowsing among the pure uniforms,

the spotless knobs of the machines.
Because the dry, unearthly air
consoles you, though the white clothes
struggle through the ozone to set you free.

NEAR SOLON, IOWA

Snow falls into the world
from the rim of darkness;

we drive out into it,
the farms passing us

like places we played,
like places we thought we would live.

In the steep confusion of the air
the animals lie down and the barns sleep

over their graves in the fields.
The slippery road, the town we come to

with its gas stations closed:
it is time to go home.

We mark a driveway with our tire tracks.
The house is dark but for the

snow on its roof; we do not live there.
And taking the same way back,

we watch through the windshield
the cold wheels turning above the road,

the slow spokes of the sky.
Sleep drives us home.

THE NORTH

Quartz, rockets: memory tampers
with this simple sky, turning it
into things. It is the cockpit,

the quarry, the pocked and thrilling
universe. Try walking near it
on a night like this, with the stars

sharpening as the temperature drops,
and the drifts iced over.
If there were an accident,

you'd feel the arrow shiver
in your side, the shock of friction,
the rib crack and the roof collapse.

A blue spruce sheds its load
of snow, and each step
through the breaking crust

reminds you that you come from
here, that you belong among
the primary colors: blue, white, black.

When your fingers begin to go numb,
you go home. Nothing is kind here,
it is all durable and cold

like your lover in the kitchen
cutting up limes.

HOME FROM THE MARKET

There were house plants
with leaf rot and mites,
winter pears, thin-skinned,

in pyramids and green paper.
I bought six, brown and misshapen.
You want to eat one.

Your hand on my shoulder
hurts, love. Your urgency suggests
a hunger or a lack.

You take the groceries from me,
shove the whole bag in the icebox.
Shall I become the animal

feeding at your hand?
I forgot your oranges.
I daydreamed down the aisles

of scarabs, tomb jewelry, and seeds,
dry and preserved, like rice in boxes.
Also of necklaces, of their weight,

and of grinding malachite
for eye paint. Roughness
becomes you, when I need roughness.

Feel what a temperature
my face stores,
in from the cold.

It is no accident you bruise
my neck, and say my name
as though it hurts.

BITTERNESS AND RUE

Having had too many drinks,
I hold to the road with second sight.
Nothing is sobering,
not the first close call,
not the sirens for someone else.
Nothing enters but the sad piano
played for me tonight,
one blessing, from the local station.
I drive to wake myself
from a man as feverless as milk,
that mild and common soporific.
No one will argue with me about
bitterness, sleek cat with a bird,
or about hunger, my other animal.

His face is like the first, clear
lubricating drop. It can't be taken back.
Pain has had its way with him,
trading in hardness.
No door opening, no flowers.
He sits at a table reading,
a window behind his head.
I watch the white crysanthemums
drift past, tender places in the sky
that open and open.
He is a green branch divining for water,
water he will find, and fear.
He says our species should not propagate,
but he shudders as the young horse
shudders in the rain,
with a spasm of exposure.

GEODE

The birds start up,
and noisily the big branches

dip and shudder.
He lies with the blanket

kicked away, his head in grass
lit with a dark glitter of dew.

I should shake him.
The sky, which is liquid and black,

will drain to the blue dregs.
Sleep is a subtraction.

The clean wind comes to his forehead
and not to mine. Therefore,

we live on the extract, the twilight:
one loves to watch the other sleeping.

The stars will survive us, like a pox.
They try to prick us now.

In spite of myself, I love the hard spark.
The white pine sends down

its cool medicine. I kiss his mouth.
Morning cracks,

the geode with its brain of quartz.

NORTHERN LIGHTS

I soak the clothes,
cold water a relief,
and slump in the hammock

peeling an orange, throwing the peels
into the coiled green garden hose.
The lights start up again.

We don't need them.
A plump bird spits in the oven,
dripping fat. Upstairs,

you're typing again: work noise,
the slow fan, a fine sweat
on your skin. I yell, *want anything?*

but you don't hear. From the road,
the smell of gasoline.
No one told us it was alarming,

this attrition,
this chafing of cold, unironed sheets,
or that the sky whips itself for us:

clean pink welts, the sting of infection.
It steeps our house in its ray-light:
the woman fixed in her hammock,

the man who pretends to himself
he comforts her,
who does comfort her.

THIS WAS A FARM

This was a farm. A tractor
without tires rusts in the yard.
Did we come, clothes full of burrs,
to be saddened by the house,
its roof buckled, collapsing?

Or to listen for ourselves
in the whine of the coiled wire?
Whole panes unbroken. The world
flowers in the inward pink
convolutions of the sky;

hay without color thrashes
around us, and no cattle
drink at the metal basins.
We could become this, complete
as the barn doors opening,

banging, opening, banging.
All we have to do is stay.
Live here. Give up everything.
Never speak, or sleep. Even
now, the memory flinches

within us, and we long for
a home in the cold, stopped light,
the salt licks, the barn. See how
the roof takes fire, kindling the
sun and corrugated tin.

RENO

Women love emotions.
One by one we appear
in the palace of machinery and lights
as though fresh from spa waters,
and stroll through the tourists
enthralled by the elegant flow
of money out of their lives.
They are underdressed for the desert
this time of year.
In the glittering aisles,
the stars and cherries
whirl on their spools
and do not align.
Parts of heaven must be
that mathematical,
since some minds are uncomfortable
off in the billows,
where it is too soft.
I am not distracted by emotion.
I use it. A cold man is an inspiration.
So I appear excitable, unhinged,
and sit at a table of perfect green,
and win. Love is a country
to which we return and return,
but in which we cannot live.

LAKE SURPRISE

The spruces are much too personal.
At this altitude,
even the rife, anonymous flowers
have names that are symbols of something,
or so she tells me,
including one I'm certain she invented:
those blue ones, "Heaven's Spies."

We've walked on snow for an hour at least,
on the source of snow, which is melting.
How can a glacier
pour itself away beneath our feet
and still be somewhat permanent?

I cup the icy run-off in my hands
and drink, and what I drink
recalls the stony well
that held the constellations,
which Father said were the lights
in God's house, and to go to sleep.

I am "a man reluctant to kiss in public"
according to her, and what of it?
Even climbing becomes too personal:
her sweater with its arms around her waist,
and her assertion that fate
is a kind of parking ticket
in my case, since I attach it to misdeeds.

God sees people who kiss in public,
and flowers are only flowers, even this high,
though the view of her is startling,
stopped so suddenly by the lake, our destination,
as though appalled by its color
or its cloud-breath against her.

If only I could doze a while
near the shocking water,
or in its strict reflection,
I might be free of pronouns while I slept.

SNOW LIGHT

I stop, winded, the air sifting down.
Here is the peculiar light I hoped for.
The branches of the pines are lobed with snow,
each shape intact, and brightened from within.

I walked among these flickering trunks in fall,
the grass grown stiff and noisy underfoot,
and found a mystery, a tree, a flowering quince,
all pale and fragrant, out of season.

It gave off this light.
What is holy is earth's unearthliness.
Love, could we describe it,
would break apart, lucency and force.

A starling rasps from his white precinct.
Far back in the woods, the snow is falling again,
perhaps into your life. The wind returns
to chisel its drifts and ribbing.

Forgive the rounded burdens of the branches.
They do not suffer, suffused in this light.
They are not sorrows,
though that is the meaning we give them.

AGAINST THE COLD

August, that outlaw, loosens the stars.
They fall suddenly, a long way,
and hold us in a deep exposure,
so the wish comes too late.
Then the sky closes.

Even the drastic clarity of winter stars
cannot disturb us so completely.
Traveling alone, a wish would go numb
up there, propelled by sheer cold.
It would never return.

Wishes do not return.
Love comes of its own accord,
as the cactus blooms by itself
in the drowsy greenhouse, suddenly and once,
or as nipples harden

out of cold or desire,
suddenly and many times.
In the spring, the melting wind
abandons its souvenirs, debris of flowers,
and on the radio the polkas

inflict their harmless sadness.
A man on a ladder paints his house.
The muscles of his back
make another ladder, salty and edible.
The wish might be for the sound

of the five snaps on his shirt letting go.
Someone might say such wishes
were a bad bet, like raising the stakes
for the pure joy of risk,
pushing your money forward.

With so many stars strewn around
and burning, who could hold back?
Night-blue heaven sheds parts of itself.
Some reach the earth:
hard light from the stars, windfall.

WHAT THE QUEEN SAYS
(Five Card Stud)

The company I keep
is mixed, at best.
Sometimes it's riffraff and boys,
a slick Jack, or worse.
Sometimes—you know the odds—
the rare one comes,
the purebred, sureheaded one
that changes you.
The sequence falls so certainly
around you, it seems unclear
how you arrived there,
or how, at that one moment,
it overtook you.
Sometimes the story
lasts in the talk for a while—
a hand like that.
Me, I admire the ones
who call it quits,
who know what enough is.
They fold for the night
and go home to someone
who reads in bed.
I had enough, and I lost it.
I'll have it and lose it again.

THE IRIS, THAT SEXUAL FLOWER

The iris, that sexual flower,
holds itself closed.
The florist's bucket is blue
with closed flowers:
bunches of irises
wet with their sap
printing the eyes.
The tongue in the mouth
knows the blueprint,
the promise: the tongue on the neck.

The stems in the pail swim downward,
pulling up water. Water's the weight
of the swimmer, the eyelids,
the cords of the neck,
the collarbone, wishbone,
the speaking power of the mouth.
A kiss gives the mouth a drink.
Give me a drink.
The blue iris opens in the heart,
that bucket, in sexual water.

PHYSICS

Think of the present as a splitting atom,
one-half weighted, out of kilter,
trailing its roots and trash,
and then the liquid glamour of the other,
swimming forward into foreign darkness
and the soft folds of space.
If fate is a chromosome,
a man and a woman might be
capable of genetic love.

No one leaves for heaven anymore,
that ill-lit, inhospitable
planet the color of eggshell,
sick with candles and flowers.
It empties itself of all things outlandish,
that is its purpose.
It crushes the fossil stars
for its fuel, clogging the sky
with their dessicated seed.

One human body, female, shudders.
Think of her pleasure as a tiny engine
or a unit of generated energy.
As something for nothing.
All over the earth the separate sparks
flash quietly, with exquisite frailty.
A body holding more of a charge
would come apart like the fractured atom,
and heaven, inverted, be used
as a bin for the debris.

When the music forces sadness on us,
the coincidence of joy unnerves us,
and the sexual lights flare up,
we drift into a universe of disasters
holding our slight, impractical instruments,
navigating by instinct,
as though that could save us.

You know what happens.
We survive straight through to the end.
We lie down together
on a hard, familiar bed
though each of us has been
already once or twice
a godsend to someone else.
Let love infect and reinfect us,
and endure in our blood
as a code of bright cells,
holy and incurable.

THE FROZEN RIVER

This could be drawn without a single curve,
the surface broken, driven upward.
Triangle, rectangle, the steep light falls
over the river's panes, and clings.

Who could hold water in a vise?

The cracking comes from within, from
an open place where sunlight heats the stones
and my family bathes in the cool water.
My young mother, my father restored.

HERE

Rumpled and calm, you sleep like a boy,
your hand upturned near the fruit

in the bowl, as though sleep and hunger
had quarreled, and sleep won.

You are far away as a word at large,
tip of the tongue,

and will not be recalled.
I remember you five years ago, six.

No, not you. Another man—
tar, the sound of construction,

and his motorcycle snarling up the trail,
the dirt ruts. And me picking raspberries

all afternoon, dropping them into your old hat.
His, I mean. Soft brim.

Someone has come to the window or door,
someone who will not answer.

Father? The sleet begins;
the partridge stiffen in their canvas sack.

We are crossing snow patches, hunting.
The soft-mouthed dogs fetch the warm birds,

and everywhere there is brittle grass
and the too-thin ice of streams.

And now the slanted shutters of the beach house,
old bathing caps, Grandmother's big towels.

I'm twelve, skinny and upset,
lying on the hot flagstones.

What are you doing here,
standing, still half-asleep,

your mouth full of cold,
red-black cherries?

THE DARK HINGES

You call the cardinals. They answer,
but keep their distance.
They flash through the birches and barbed wire:
red darts, explicit song.
Their private lives intrigue you.

About clouds you care less.
To you, they are less human and today
you ignore their white Rorschach
and watch the birds.

Fish also intrigue you.
You know their habits, and know
that to bring that wet silver
into our world, you must go down
with your mind into the stroking weeds,
and you are prepared to.

Now in a boat you move away,
dipping the oars. The new shellac
lights up the wood. It is evening,
it is morning. The farther you are,
the slower. You could be at your piano,
bone on bone. The complaint of the geese
might also be yours, that faint barking.

You row away, the remnant of your face
struck by the northern light
like the undersides of the torn leaves
in the steep woods after the rain.
The loon between us is our borderland,
unnerving mercy from a mile across the water.
Are you an animal,
your thumb against the reel

that clicks off water beads?
The clouded territory of the fish,
the lucent run-off, neither light nor sky,
where the geese passed through—
these are the dark hinges between lives.

JAKE'S TURTLE

He remembers his mother
in an orange dress,
walking to the gate, alarmed.
His father stood uncertainly
with a weight on his pitchfork:
the turtle. Jake remembers the prongs'
bloodless holes in the throat,
the closed face, the small and rubbery tail.

One by one he fills the glasses with wine,
the whole circumference of the table.
His mother did these things.
Fixed the flowers, as he fixes them.
Tiger lilies, startling flowers,
the color of her dress.

The guests arrive, and he talks
of that day, how the sky filled
with blue-black clouds, tender and clean.
She is like the letter fallen
into the mailbox by mistake.
So Jake goes on and on about the turtle,
its underside of black and yellow octagons,
its still surprising weight.
He will make a grave for it,
and tend it. He loves the dead,
and keeps their anniversaries.

YOUR EIGHTIETH

There is death in old postcards,
death in the sack of trash.
The future of the house is overgrown.
You mention it, the briars at the screens.
The sky reminds you of the sky
in your childhood, before thunder.
Even then, the white pines shook
and darkened, as though great birds
had come to roost in them.
The west wind opens, and water
streams out into the world,
though to hear you tell it,
we're in for a drought.
More fires, and the river is lower.
Your shawl has slipped from your bones again.
The arms wave me away.
You make a fragile music
with the ice in your glass.
Bourbon is your next-to-last reward.
The rugged flapping in the thick boughs
could be the wind come to fetch you,
or angels with a family likeness,
their powerful, averted faces
stiff with human love for you.

THREE DREAMS OF DISASTER

A bank of cumulonimbus,
strangely colored, above trees.
A mountain in semidarkness,
stony, through binoculars.
Someone said,
"Look up, where the dogs are looking."
The dogs ran ahead, diminutive in the lenses,
into a place without oxygen,
void of life and perfectly beautiful.

The sea sucked all its water away,
forsaking its billion shuddering fish
and the hopeless octopus heaving
in unnatural gravity.
Shellfish colonies dried, losing their colors.
The sea betrayed its mysteries,
and gave up its favors to anyone.
On the cliffs, a liar told the crowds
a convincing theory of physics.

It was the season for falling stars.
Even so, too many cars with open doors
were stopped on a back road, on a clear night.
Stars were falling. But why such silence,
why quiet the children? Then we drowned
in the cold thrill of science fiction.
It was exquisite, the white dust blown
from a whole portion of the sky
while we felt nothing, and nothing else changed.

THE DIM PARADE

The dogs have dragged a deer's head
into the yard. The neck bone points
to the raw east, where the sun
pries light from a cloud.
Summer, the bitter black lips.

To escape this we drive all day
through towns that disturb us,
their windows full of dust.
Who whistles in the woods?
We begin to pass houses that fascinate.

Some sadness is inherited. Not all sadness.
These houses have a certain look,
as though the lives inside them
were stenciled, one over another.
Even the barns that redden in the rain
hold nothing but lives halfway to the boneyard,
horses and cattle and those that feed them.
And so we drive, to pass the dim parade.

Some pain is instructive. Not all pain.
Next to the blackening gardens
and rooms that darken,
heaven is a white place.
A matted cow, showing her ribs,
turns her single, delicate horn toward us.
She stands in withered grass,
in a field bathed by storm light.
Such frail tinder.
Warfare makes that black and white debris.

In the town of white stones,
a tractor cuts the tall grass
soundlessly, and the rain soaks down
into the cold compartments, the honeycomb.
Mown grass is the scent of the dead.

THE CHEMIST AND HIS DAUGHTER

Up here, the bottles shine.
Starved for a grain of sleep,
I squint at labels,
handwritten labels, her work.
This bathrobe used to fit;
now I hardly find my hands.
She says my soul takes up the room.
Women, with their mollifying lies.

This will be my heaven, these shelves
of scales and weights and pills.
Damn her,
she knows I'm fumbling with the lids.
And damn my caliper hands,
the bones have curved.
There she goes, half-dark with her drink,
out onto the lawn.
She'll call to me, or to the window.
Always repeats herself.
Something about a birthday,
I don't remember.
Women, with their anniversaries.

I want to sleep. Music from her party
might make me dream.
I could dance the ladies round,
except for the dizziness.
                         She's on the stairs.
Sometimes she shines like Christmas night,
that girl, yellow and talkative.
And sometimes dark, enclosed,
and serious, like medicine,
she'll come to my bedside
with news, a blanket, or a tray,
or the minerals I take to stave off colds.

LIKE A CARETAKER

I live here, but do not live here.
Trash blows through the sky tonight.
Out of a snowy tree, the stars appear,

drops of ice water, they seem so pure.
The tree petrifies. They are its parasites.
I live here, but do not live here.

"Fusion" was the word I loved—its nuclear
logic. The world with a heart of dynamite.
Out of a snowy tree, the stars appear

faceted and cold, an elegant prayer
addressed to death. Death loves black and white.
I live here, but do not live here.

Creatures are born from atoms, from air
parentless, and drift like satellites
out of a snowy tree. The stars appear

to be parts of a machine in disrepair,
which I do not repair. And for this oversight,
I live here, but do not live here.
Out of a snowy tree, the stars appear.

NOSTALGIA FOR THE FUTURE

A cold joy leaps from the orchard
in early evening,
when the pear and apple flower.
Their petals enclose
the nubs of the unformed fruits
with a private dampness.
Cattle drift through the fields
like headstones, and soon
the sky will spill its milky light
down almost into the trees.

Children are swimming
in a limestone pool
under other trees.
Clouded and still, the water
passes from white to dark
without a trace of blueness.
Each pale body liquifies.
Down in the dark part
near the drain,
the drowned frogs turn
in their underwater afterlife,
spreading their tiny fingers.

A man winds his watch
in the merciful near-dark.
He lies on a mound of soft grasses,
this year's and last year's,
in the orchard of scent and wetness.
His children have slept
past their births.
They swim in the trees
among lime-pale flowers.

46

His story is sad and ordinary.
The ghosts in the leaves
are telling it again:
the beautiful towns of childhood,
the marriages and deaths.
Disconsolate, they are always
coming and going away,
fluttering the limpid pear flowers.
Disturbed by the color
of clouds at night,
and stung by the minor lights
of the fireflies,
they whisper their longing.
Unkissed, their mouths are hard
and tender as the final pear.

WATERCRESS & ICE

The grass gave way, and suddenly
you were thigh-deep in water so cold
it made you forget yourself.
You saw two wild blue herons,
and mention these things in your letter.
The brilliant, green-white substance
you walked through was watercress,
watercress and ice. I can see you,
underdressed, wading out
into the breakable, ice-invaded plants.

I cut these lilacs from the wet hedge
half-bloomed, cold to the touch.
Their fragrance has none of the
delicious bitterness you walk through.
The transient herons have gone,
taking their blue lives home.
It's a northerner's story to be cold,
though you know we unfold our maps
with explicit tenderness.
And the lilacs are bitterly beautiful,
opening already in the warm room,
purple and simple,
because I make you see them.
We will not find the wilderness
where we expect it,
nor find, in cold, a home.

WHEN THE RAPTURE COMES,
I WILL DEPART EARTH
(Sign seen in a car window in Kansas)

The earth does not end in the pink sky.
It is not a room with a wall lit by candles.
Nor does it end in the body,
in your hands upon the wheel,
or in the sexual backache of driving.

What should we pray
to the smoke and bone of the grass?
That its death light our way into otherness?
As if its color flowed from a silver tube
we could uncap and empty?

Above the road, the yellow leaves
enter the hereafter. They are almost gone.
No death in the sweet, pink sky
could stun us with such clarity.
Not even the permanent flowers of the clouds.

When the rapture comes,
let the car continue through the woods
unharmed by miracles.
And if a fierce, atomic heaven falls,
let it stop us in an ordinary act.

49

THE FIRST SNOW

Autumn now tenders an exquisite raggedness,
and the apples clench into the pure flavors
of cider and a season beneath the snow.
The wavering, sinuous V's of Canada geese
contract and relax in the whitening sky.
Of the first snow, the weatherman says,
"thank heaven it's drifting slowly northward,"
meaning out of our region, as if into heaven,
which the blade of your compass strains for,
and which my heart, compressed by an emotion
close to arousal, strains for also.
Heaven must lie to the north. Its light
comes down to us through a crack in the world
at dawn and twilight, and on the occasion
of snowfall and hurricane, and even at night
it roams across the sky in the hard colors
of the north, liquid and stroking.

Our window opens into it. This time
it takes the form of darkness left ajar,
for trees that clot with falling snow appear,
and drift beside us in a thick light.
Flake and grain build to a particular brilliance
bound by the tensile strength of itself.
And this begun in a sky empty of everything
but moisture and temperature, out of which
the white tumult finally rouses.
The muscular tension in the drifts
is the traction of the poles, you to me to you.
What starts as heaven drawn to itself ends
as the slow upheaval of your body in mine.

THE BILLOWING LIGHTS

Someone appears
in the trackless, floating field,
a body the color of cloud,
or the gauze that's
slowly stripped away
after sleep or sex,
or genuine pain.
It is a soul
who cautiously looks down,
deciding to stay
in the changeable vapors,
small and unborn,
abstract as a crystal,
and have that be its life.

Where they are,
they are safe from fire
and the transforming cold,
safe from money.
And yet,
in certain kinds of weather,
they draw near
as if for comfort,
as people are drawn
to a snowy, foreign place
after marriage or a loss.
They press into the leaves
of trees made explicit by rain,
there in the radiant dark
like a black migration.
Or quite overtly
in a day of blindness,
they come close
to ask for something,

but all we hear
is the dry snow,
its whispering friction,
and the scraping
engines of the plows.

Perhaps it is the sexual
dream they long for,
the ways we have
of thwarting the filthy rains,
and blood and age.
They may come down
out of the sorrowful air,
lured by the billowing
lights of wars
like fish to inedible glitter,
that longing the one
force of their lives.

They peer down
into the earthly light,
the delicate towns
burning in the radium
of the future,
and the white air falling.
Little fossil ghosts,
they grow dim and quiet,
embedded in the sky.
And tonight, to keep them
from the slicing wind,
I do not want them.

HIS CAMERA

The brain is not the mind. The fire door bangs
above the white apartment of your friend,
the weeping figs and delicate ammonia of the Brie.
Each stone of the roof is a block of cold
glamorous as pale new firewood piled
against the clouds, towers, and stars,
while below, the braided lights of the avenues
twist and evolve, pearls and amber beads
with a crust of gold. It is winter
in an age of science and music.

We stand like relatives, or two foreigners
faced with the same strange world.
The darkness we drink holds a binding chill.
Is tenderness something mechanical?
For I love the swift abstraction with which
you look around you for the critical light,
tender and mortal in your hat and coat.
Your camera quietly stutters in your hands,
mindless, but the mechanism by which
these moments become durable, one after another.

HOLY NIGHT

The land loved by the dead
is the forest after the fire,
when rain is a silt of ash
and the sky a stony field.

The poor do not love it,
stubborn among the white
crushed leaves, which disintegrate,
giving off the faint scent of money.

Animals range just out of sight
into the deepening meadows,
the moon on their backs.
They graze in paradise.

The dead walk in a wood
of charcoal and prayer,
eating light for their communion,
clothed in the hard-won, elegant clouds.

But the prayers of the poor
are thrust like the white leaves upward
toward the peace of God,
which passeth human understanding.

Minnows and grasses are the same
to the dead, numerous reflecting spirits.
And the field is a mirror in paradise,
and life a moment.

But the poor, who dwell forever
in the moment of life, are afraid.
To them, the central stone in the sky
is a pit of water.

The paper boats of their prayers
are blown by a breath that fails.
Animals drink in the monochromatic lake,
and feed on the moon's gray grasses.

THE CACTUS IS THE LESSON

Bone structure of a boat
scoured by the wind's pumice
suspends in the dark boathouse,
glistening with salt.
Rain sweetens the ropes and nets.
Tides of sand have pocked
the spiny plants, which burst
from the hard grains
uncalled for, succulent.
Far out on the horizon,
mirages of boats
appear and reappear
through sheets of water.
The sky is a cold mauve
washed from the sea.

A cactus flowers on our table,
the drop of color among the spikes
lucid as the jewel
on the waiter's hand.
Dreamily the light shifts
through the glass and silver,
falling from far above
onto the pink tablecloths.
A fish you call "staggeringly beautiful"
curves like a weapon in the pan,
its sharp fin exposed,
arranged in its colors and juices
among green sprigs
and the spiral twists of lemons.
Rainy light fills our glasses.
The world glimmers
like a wreck in the sea.

GRACE

The sky breaks into furrows
darker than the color of peaches,
rough as a newly ploughed field.
Birds are the black seed
scattered there. Deep
in the woods of fattening buds,
a wall that once
divided field from field
softens with mosses,
though the stones in its center
still keep the cold.
Pits, seeds, and kernels
split in the cool dirt
under the half-thawed leaves.
The honeysuckle will unwind
on the fences, the faint orange
in the tight flowers
suggesting itself in the sky.
A window will be forced
open in the heart,
and the clouds will swell
and tilt with honey,
each flower a translucent
basin of light
that brims and overflows.

HIS SHOULDERS IN THE WATER

He swims into the reflections of clouds,
the purple, plantless depth
of the space between them.
The specific poisons of insects
have raised a dozen welts on his back,
which he soothes in the cold anesthesia
of a lake without boat or dock.
In early spring the windows of the cottages
fill with the sky's white musculature.
Shadowy lilacs move around them,
gray-blue, uncorrupted by children.
No rough towels dry on the grass.
His shoulders shudder in the water,
embracing and letting go,
striped by the ladders of cold
down which he could climb
into the intimate currents
where the dead swim, half-awake
and slippery with memory.
All around him they rise
to feed on the particles
of light his pale feet leave,
thrashing in the part of the sky
that is moving away
and yet always here.

STARKWEATHER HOUSE

How heavy the trees are with rain,
like trees from another century.

A pound of droplets weighs down
each branch of the lilac,

doubling the weight of its scent.
Above the wet meadow, the crows

float with surprising dignity,
or preen on the slate roof

which is speckled with lichens.
Whoever planted the white flowers

is dead now, with flowers on his grave.
And in the house, whoever wound the clocks

when they were new is dead,
though the clocks tick and chime

in the front hall, where pollen drops
onto the black table and is left there

because the yellow dust is pleasing
to those who are alive.

Someone who loved lilies
chose the paper on these walls,

silver and brown, as calming
as rain, or a glass of wine.

There is a breakdown in the cells
that improves everything,

makes men most delicious in their forties,
the plum when only a tension of the skin

holds in the juice. Did a man stand
in an upstairs room, looking out over

the leafy debris in the gutters
on a fallen evening like this?

Light curved among the slates
that reminded him of fish scales,

and his loneliness returned, a tender pain,
as he thought of the age of his parents.

The whole house smelled of cut flowers.
The crows shook out their ragged wings.

FRANZ, THE WORLD IS ABSTRACT

They stroked me with white dust,
as though I should feel at home with dryness!
And in the fields around the house,
crickets produced a steady joy from friction.
I was a fish in the watery gleam,
dawn with its lake-light.
My window opened into the sky,
and I was consoled by the hugeness,
and the comfortable movements of the trees.

When I fell asleep,
I knew my world would leave me.
Sleep is full of comings and goings:
the queer, expressive faces of my parents,
the new thrill of rain.
Bending over the white crib,
my father says—and why so sadly?—
"Franz, the world is abstract,"
and I do not know what he means.

What they find lovely, meaningful, and sad,
is all I've ever known.
The surface of the lake distressed by wind
like thousands of pages riffled and turned,
or my mother on her haunches
in a heavy sweater, feeding the sweet,
thick fire with balsam twigs
on a cold morning when the year is ill.
The sumac's red spears.

Even now, as sleep consumes me
(for things happen without us in this world),
the pure, anachronistic flowers
of the hydrangea undo me, the bitter leaves.

61

My parents fret about the dead.
So many have died,
and we do not know where they are.
I thought they were fish in the river,
and close at hand, but I forget.

WEBSTER'S SECOND

A scent like that of sherry
comes to him. He broods
over the dictionary,
the small black pictures
of the world the way it was,
lost like the carved stones
that lie beneath the rose brambles.
A queer light falls on his desk.
It comes to him:
the alcohol in the fallen apples,
the darkening blue that thunders.
The pages are Bible-thin,
near-transparent,
and bring to his mind
the complex cold circles
of the Cedar River,
which he sometimes wades in.

Before his son was born,
the fans whirled all summer,
even at night. His dog
lounged in the cool rhubarb
as if in shallow water,
while dust and fertilizers
circled above the road.
stirred up by nothing.
And early in the evenings,
the children of the neighborhood
occurred in the faultless light
and played until the world
filled up with shadows.
He heard their cries,
the cracking bat,

but he could not believe
that they were real.
They were the subtle ghosts
a camera catches above ground.
They pulsed in the twilight
like fireflies.
It was the damp grass
that pained him, and the abandoned
bodies of their bicycles.

The dog travels a circle of dirt
on his rope, smelling the thunder.
The tremors appear
in the bright paper seed-packets
speared into the black garden,
and in the surface of the cold beer
in his glass, and the empty clothesline
with its dangling wooden pins.
His wife lifts his son, who struggles,
into her arms. She will bring
the thankful dog in from the rain.
In the cool, pellucid pages on his desk,
apples drop from the heavy tree
into the other world.
He sees the multiplying rain,
their house tinged with violet light,
and the whole Midwest
far gone in its elegant dilapidation,
unfurling like the once-luminous roses,
loose now at their centers,
which cause such a thrilling sadness.

PITT POETRY SERIES

Ed Ochester, General Editor

Dannie Abse, *Collected Poems*
Adonis, *The Blood of Adonis*
Jack Anderson, *Toward the Liberation of the Left Hand*
Jon Anderson, *Death & Friends*
Jon Anderson, *In Sepia*
Jon Anderson, *Looking for Jonathan*
John Balaban, *After Our War*
Gerald W. Barrax, *Another Kind of Rain*
Michael Benedikt, *The Badminton at Great Barrington; Or, Gustave Mahler & the Chattanooga Choo-Choo*
Lorna Dee Cervantes, *Emplumada*
Robert Coles, *A Festering Sweetness: Poems of American People*
Leo Connellan, *First Selected Poems*
Fazıl Hüsnü Dağlarca, *Selected Poems*
Norman Dubie, *Alehouse Sonnets*
Norman Dubie, *In the Dead of the Night*
Stuart Dybek, *Brass Knuckles*
Odysseus Elytis, *The Axion Esti*
John Engels, *Blood Mountain*
John Engels, *Signals from the Safety Coffin*
Brendan Galvin, *The Minutes No One Owns*
Brendan Galvin, *No Time for Good Reasons*
Gary Gildner, *Digging for Indians*
Gary Gildner, *First Practice*
Gary Gildner, *Nails*
Gary Gildner, *The Runner*
Mark Halperin, *Backroads*
Patricia Hampl, *Woman Before an Aquarium*
Michael S. Harper, *Song: I Want a Witness*
John Hart, *The Climbers*
Samuel Hazo, *Blood Rights*
Samuel Hazo, *Once for the Last Bandit: New and Previous Poems*
Samuel Hazo, *Quartered*
Gwen Head, *Special Effects*
Gwen Head, *The Ten Thousandth Night*
Milne Holton and Graham W. Reid, eds., *Reading the Ashes: An Anthology of the Poetry of Modern Macedonia*
Milne Holton and Paul Vangelisti, eds., *The New Polish Poetry: A Bilingual Collection*
David Huddle, *Paper Boy*

Shirley Kaufman, *The Floor Keeps Turning*
Shirley Kaufman, *From One Life to Another*
Shirley Kaufman, *Gold Country*
Ted Kooser, *Sure Signs: New and Selected Poems*
Abba Kovner, *A Canopy in the Desert: Selected Poems*
Paul-Marie Lapointe, *The Terror of the Snows: Selected Poems*
Larry Levis, *Wrecking Crew*
Jim Lindsey, *In Lieu of Mecca*
Tom Lowenstein, tr., *Eskimo Poems from Canada and Greenland*
Archibald MacLeish, *The Great American Fourth of July Parade*
Peter Meinke, *The Night Train and The Golden Bird*
Peter Meinke, *Trying to Surprise God*
Judith Minty, *In the Presence of Mothers*
James Moore, *The New Body*
Carol Muske, *Camouflage*
Leonard Nathan, *Dear Blood*
Sharon Olds, *Satan Says*
Gregory Pape, *Border Crossings*
Thomas Rabbitt, *Exile*
Ed Roberson, *Etai-Eken*
Ed Roberson, *When Thy King Is A Boy*
Eugene Ruggles, *The Lifeguard in the Snow*
Dennis Scott, *Uncle Time*
Herbert Scott, *Groceries*
Richard Shelton, *The Bus to Veracruz*
Richard Shelton, *Of All the Dirty Words*
Richard Shelton, *You Can't Have Everything*
Gary Soto, *The Elements of San Joaquin*
Gary Soto, *The Tale of Sunlight*
David Steingass, *American Handbook*
Tomas Tranströmer, *Windows & Stones: Selected Poems*
Alberta T. Turner, *Learning to Count*
Alberta T. Turner, *Lid and Spoon*
Chase Twichell, *Northern Spy*
Constance Urdang, *The Lone Woman and Others*
Cary Waterman, *The Salamander Migration and Other Poems*
Bruce Weigl, *A Romance*
David P. Young, *The Names of a Hare in English*
David P. Young, *Sweating Out the Winter*